FRANCESCO PAOLO MAULUCCI

The National Archaeological Museum of Naples

PUBLISHER CARCAVALLO-NAPLES

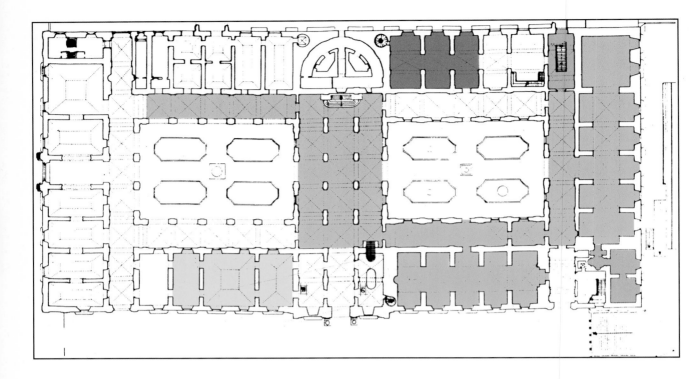

Ground Floor

SCULPTURES

GEMS

LECTURE HALL

EXHIBITION AREA

ACCESS TO EGYPTIAN COLLECTION

ACCESS TO EPIGRAPH COLLECTION

Basement Floor

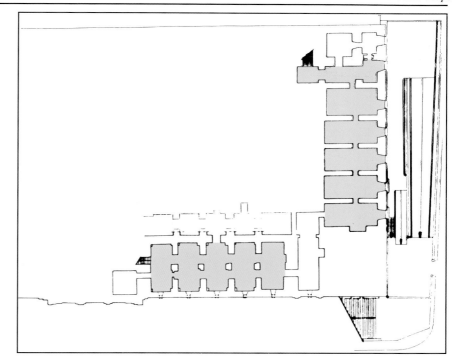

EGYPTIAN
COLLECTION

EPIGRAPH
COLLECTION

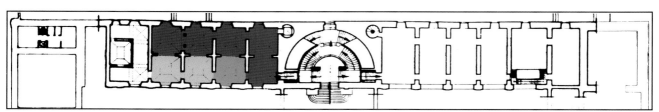

Mezzanine Floor

MOSAICS

SCULPTURES

ASTARITA COLLECTION

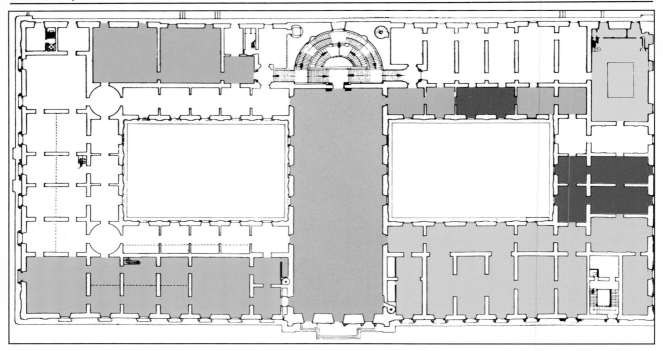

First Floor

                              Atlas Room

                              Pompeii Painting Room
Room of Italian Painting
Room of Campania Painting and Architectural Decoration
Room of Boscoreale II Style Painting
Room of Campania, Mythological, Epic and Pompeii Painting
Room of Pompeii Painting with the origins of Rome
Room of Pompeii Painting with landscapes, portraits and costume scenes
Room of Painting of the Villa of Agrippa Postumo

                              Room of Italic and Roman Bronze Weapons

                              Ivory and Glazed Terracotta Room
Coloured Glassware Room - Silver Room
Pottery Room

                              Villa of Scrolls

                              Relief model of Pompeii

                              Prehistoric and protohistoric collection

                              Isis Temple

Orpheus and Eurydice, bas-relief of unknown prov., Pentelic marble, 1.18 x 1.00 m.

Orpheus and Eurydice

Orpheus, the mythical singer who with the divine sound of his lyre opened the doors of Hades, in order to win back his beloved wife, immaturely descended to Hell, and to take her back to the kingdom of the living, had to comply with only one condition imposed by Zeus: during the return journey he should not look back at his beloved Eurydice. But, forgetting the condition and transported by his feelings, Orpheus looked back at her and lost her again for ever.

The tragic moment of the final good-bye is the theme of this bas-relief of Augustan period, considered with two others (the myth of Peliades and that of Hercules letting Theseus and Pirithus free from Hades) to be the frieze of a tomb or of a choragic monument for theatrical victories. As a matter of fact the marble, the only copy among the three referable to a Phidian original, having the names of the people (from left to right Hermes, Eurydice, Orpheus) engraved in Greek, is considered one of the masterpieces of the Museum for the high quality and delicacy of execution, and the recomposition of the various fragments does not spoil it. The tragic fact of the married couple, in which the same Hermes seems to take part, and who appears to suffer an inner torment because of the unescapable task entrusted to him of bringing Eurydice back, is lived with chaste parsimony of gestures and words where hidden pain has already turned to a deep sorrow. There is neither rage nor rebellion against the will of Zeus and also the lyre which performed the miracle is still hanging from Orpheus' left hand as a dear object. The consciousness or remorse for having failed and the lost hope of ever seeing the light again after the darkness, leave both the protagonists little room for the slightest gesture of leavetaking. Not even that of Hermes who again approaches Eurydice, holding her right hand delicately with his left, is an impatient gesture, because he also is overcome by deep emotion and he seems to grant them a moment or two more. But the movements indicate that time is pressing, they all know it and most of all Eurydice: her right foot, unlike her body, is already ready, the irremediable has happened, they must go.

A Short History of the Building and of its Collections

Statue of a daughter of M.N. Balbo, prov. Herculaneum, Basilica, marble 1.80 m.

Almost as if predestined for this purpose, the building later used as the National Museum of Naples, was built on an archaeologically interesting site, i. e. at the foot of Santa Teresa Hill, not far from a Greek cemetery on which was the garden of the monastery of the Theresian Fathers. Numerous vases, in fact, come from it; some of them belonged later to the queen Caroline Murat, some remained in the Museum.

The work of the earlier building, carried out between 1582 and 1586 by order of the Spanish Viceroy Don Pietro Giran Duke of Ossuna, and designed by the architect Giulio Cesare Fontana aimed at raising the Royal Riding School. But when they realized that in that place there was no water for the horses, the stable was moved near the Sebeto and the old building was abandoned. The works started again between 1599 and 1601, i. e. when Don Pietro Fernandez de Castro-conte of Lemos succeeded to Ossuna, and he destined the building to the Royal University which had previously been in San Domenico Maggiore, and gave to architect Fontana the necessary mandate to carry out the required modifications. The works lasted about 15 years, until the 15th June 1615 when the Royal University was opened and where it remained until 1701. Having among its other famous teachers also Gianbattista Vico it was severely damaged by the popular riots of 1647 and by the earthquake of 1687. From 1701 in fact the history of the building became even more troubled and uncertain, as uncertain were the political matters in this part of Italy at that time. After the students had been expelled due to the Macchia Conspiracy, the building was used for tribunals and as a military barracks. But Charles III of Bourbon gave it back after restoration to the students in 1735 and they remained there until 1797, when Ferdinand IV of Bourbon, expelling the Jesuits, moved the Royal University to Ges Vecchio and the building, after some new modifications made by the architects Ferdinando Fuga and Pompeo Schiantarelli, housed the Herculaneum Museum, the Picture Gallery, the Library, the Collections of Medals and Ancient Vases, the Arts and Drawing School, the Sculpure Workshop, the Royal Painting House, the Workshops for Engravings and Restorations. Thus the first nucleus of ancient materials was constituted, although put together with some confusion, for the future Bourbon Royal Museum. But already before reaching this destination, there were in Naples two important collections of ancient things. The first one, i. e. the very famous Farnese Collection, was placed in Capodimonte Royal Palace, and, together with the interesting library, included the various works of art of different provenance, which Charles III of Bourbon inherited from his mother, Elisabetta Farnese,

Equestrian statue of M.N. Balbo, prov. Herculaneum, Basilica, marble 2.52 m.

wife of Philip V, in 1731. The second collection was placed in Portici Royal Palace, where was kept the material which came to light from the Archaeological Excavations of the little towns buried by the famous eruption of Vesuvius in 79 A. D. The history of these groups of materials is as troubled as that of the building and of course it emphasized once again the uncertain political situation of the time. In fact the Bourbons, menaced by Neapolitan patriots, euphoric for the recent victory of the Republicans in France, escaped to Palermo led by Ferdinand IV, on the 21st December, 1797, taking with them the most beautiful things of the two collections of Capodimonte and Portici. The following year the French carried away all that remained to send it to France. Fortunately, owing to wartime events, everything remained in Rome and was placed in the Farnese Palace until the return of the Bourbons to Naples in 1801, when all but the paintings returned to their place richer than before since the Marquis Venuti had bought other objects in Rome. It was different for the things taken to Palermo and others sent to that town during a second escape of the Bourbons to that city which was still under the incubus of the French, although this time the Napoleonic French. Nevertheless the loss did not seem irreparable owing to the continuous arrival of material from the Archaeological Excavations of Pompeii and Paestum and from the suppressed religious groups. Further to this, when the Museum had been rearranged and re-opened Joseph Napoleon Bonaparte reorganized its structure, adding to it the Superintendence of the Herculaneum Papyri and the Royal Academy of History and Antiquities, which in 1817 had changed its name to the Royal Bourbon Society. His work was wisely continued by Joachim Murat who had the previously mentioned Greek cemetery brought to light, and added the Borgia Museum of Velletri, containing the rich Collections of classical monuments and Egyptian antiquities collected by Giovanni Paolo Borgia in the XVIII cent., and sold by Count Borgia in 1817. In that year the Bourbons returned from the so-called "second exile", unfortunately for the penultimate time, and therefore also the material which had followed them was returned in the Museum, and declared allodial property, i. e. independent of the crown possessions, and named the Royal Bourbon Museum. Its consistence continued to increase not only thanks to the archaeological excavations in the Vesuvian cities, but also owing to the arrival of new collections. Also the collection of medals, already rich, was enlarged by the coins which had belonged to Noia, Forcella of Sicily, Baron Genova, Arditi, Poli and the historic Collection of Naples Mint. Under the dictatorship of Giuseppe Garibaldi and the following passage of power to Vittorio Emanuele II, the Museum was declared "national" and works from the suppressed monastic orders of the Community of Santa Teresa of the Barefooted and of the monumental Certosa of San Martino were added. In the meantime further purchases and generous gifts continued, among which the Collection of Cumae monuments dug up by the Count of Syracuse and bought for the Museum by the Prince of Carignano; Santangelo Museum, rich in beautiful coins bought with funds supplied by the Naples Municipium; the Palatine Collection rich in beautiful prints given by king Vittorio Emanuele II; the tapestries of the Marquis of Vasto; the collection of medals of the Mint with the historical furnishings of the Mint Workshops. In the meantime the building was cleared and the Royal Society and the Arts and Design Schools were moved elsewhere leaving only the National Library. But the need for space made it necessary to move also this in 1927 to the Royal Palace, and 30 years later, i. e. in 1957, also the Painting Collection was moved to the Capodimonte Palace, leaving the entire building for the Museum and its offices, including the Superintendence of Antiquities. After the creation of another building, at the foot of Santa Teresa Hill, connected to the main one by two transversal wings, the Museum underwent no great architectonic modification apart from the usual work of static restoration, the foundations being threatened by waterbearing strata and sismic movements which are often felt in Campania. The earthquake of 1981 caused important damage, followed by the fall of a cornice which damaged some materials returning from an exposition. As to the allocation of the building to the Museum, there have been no further interruptions, even if during the Second World War it housed the Offices of the Civil Engineers and the Medical Stores Corps with stores for sanitary materials. But after 1948 the building returned to its original function. While writing these lines great changes are being made. Apart from the usual maintenance and restoration work, in some rooms of the basement the Egyptian Collection has been shown, while, after having removed the Herculaneum Bronzes and the portraits from the Hall made available by Schiantarelli closing the arcade overlooking the left courtyard, the relevant arches are returning to their original function of portico.

Before Murat all the material remained mostly unclassified and the curator of the Museum at that time, Felice Nicholas, director also of the archaeological excavations of Pompeii and of Paestum, did not do a good job also because he was soon replaced by the Marquis Arditi, who, in spite of the numerous scientific gaps, started in 1822 to prepare an inventory of the

many objects, putting them under the following headings: Wall Paintings, Mosaics, Epigraphy, Egyptian Monuments, Marble Statues, Bas-reliefs, Bronze Animals, Small Figured Bronzes, Weapons Collection, Glass and Terracottas, Cumae Collection, Precious Objects, Medals Collection, Pornographic Objects, Right side Painting Gallery, Bronze Tools, Italian-Greek Vases, Library, Foodstuffs Collection, Papyri, Left side Paintings Gallery, Prints and Drawings. In the meantime they began publication also of a number of fine works such as "Herculaneum Antiquities" produced by the Herculaneum Academicians, while Momsen started his epigraphic study, Panofka and Gerhard began to catalogue the Museum, followed by De Iorio, Quaranta, Aloe, and Niccolini and sons who published a work in 16 volumes describing the whole Museum. Fiorelli, who was then charged with the Museum Direction and with the Archaeological Excavations of Pompeii, began publication of the Bulletin of the Museum, which soon stopped and the cataloguing with the relevant printing re-started actively. His work was revised and continued by Giulio de Petra, Paolo Orsi and Amedeo Maiuri. This latter lived through the tragic events of wartime, often taking upon himself great responsability for saving objects; as when, on two occasions, 15 June and 8 September, he drove to the Abbey of Montecassino taking several boxes containing the most precious objects of the Museum, to save them from the war; or when he walled up other precious objects in the interstices of a wall. Unfortunately the war did not save Montecassino, which became the object of terrible bombing. But, in the meantime, the boxes had been sent to the Vatican Museums and some of them to Berlin. All of them were given back on the 16th May 1946 and the 7th August 1947. A few years later, in 1949, the Museum received also a private collection. This had been realized by Marquis Marcello Spinelli who carried out the, perhaps not very scientific, archaeological excavations of the necropolis of the ancient Suessula which had been discovered on his estate. The objects found and saved from the thefts which happened very often during the war, were given to the Museum by the Marquise Elena Spinelli. They belong to the VIII-III cent. B. C.

Statue of the priestess Eumachia, prov. Pompeii, Building of Eumachia, marble, height 1.94 m.

Sarcophagus from Pozzuoli, height 1.08 m; length 2.56 m.

The Sarcophagus with the Myth of Prometheus

The creation of Man and his inevitable end in death is the magnificent theme treated in a pagan way with a complex carving on a sarcophagus found in Pozzuoli and datable not before the III cent. A.D. In fact, represented on the front of the same is the myth of Prometheus. He sits, half-naked, in the middle of the composition; in front of him the man in clay, made by him, is lying with its head on Prometheus' knees: it still lacks the breath of life. Near the figure it is possible to see, dressed in a tunic, Clotho, one of the Fates spinning the destiny of men, and a Cupid putting a lighted torch near the head of the figure in order to give it the flame of life, while with the left hand he leads towards the still body, Psyche, who is half-naked and with another bigger Cupid, trying to embrace her. He represents love, indispensable condition for life itself, which Prometheus initiated bringing to earth the fire stolen in heaven from Vulcan. This latter, in fact, is beating a piece of red hot iron on an anvil while a flying Cupid is bringing him the divine fire with a torch.

Harmodius and Aristogiton

The well known story of the Ty-
rannicides who in 514 B.C., during the Panathenaean Feasts,
layed an ambush, perhaps for
personal revenge, for the sons
of Pisistratus, Hippias and Hipparchus, despots of Athens,
without however eliminating
both of them, finds reference in
a statuary group of two naked-
men (as real heroes) representing the young Harmodius strik-
ing a blow, fatal for Hipparchus
while Aristogiton, with his left
arm stretched forward, as if to
protect his young friend, pre-
pares himself to strike a second
blow should the first one fail.

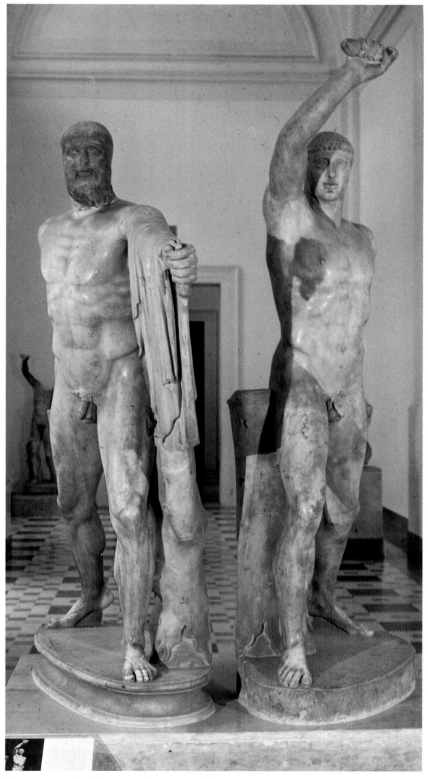

*Group of Harmodius and
Aristogiton; marble 1.95 x 2.30 m,
prov. Tivoli, Farnese Collection*

11

Athena Hygieia, prov. Farnese Collection, Greek marble, height 2.24 m.

Athena Hygieia

Dressed in an Ionic chiton, with large sleeves, over which she wears a mantle wrapped around under her left arm and buckled on the right shoulder, with the breast covered by a shield ornated with serpents and gorgons, the head covered with an Attic helmet ornated with Sphinxes and winged gryphons, from which the curly hair falls, a lance (representing lightning rending the sky) in the left hand held high, the right arm with the hand open to hold an attribute (which is missing) of perhaps an owl or a victory: this is how we see the Godess of War in all her majesty. She is not portrayed in activity but during the triumph and therefore with eyes looking down benevolently dispensing grace to the mortals, whom she seems ready to welcome with open arms.

The Lance Bearer (Doriforo)

From the Samnite Palaestra in Pompeii, where it was found in 1797, this is a copy in marble of the very famous bronze masterpiece, the Spearman of Polycletus, probably dedicated in Olympia between 450 and 440 B.C.

In this masterpiece, the Greek artist had practically expressed his theoretical study of the ideal beauty of the human body, made essentially of proportions, harmony and eurhythmy, which reveal how much the Pythagoric presuppositions were at the basis of a so defined artistic conception. Thus it provided both master and students with a canon of perfection which exceeded, according to contemporary thought, the beauty of Nature

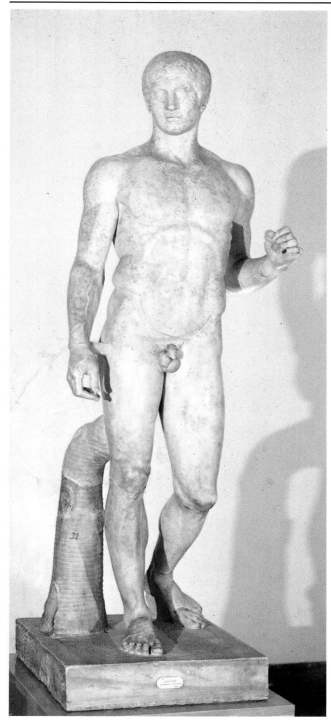

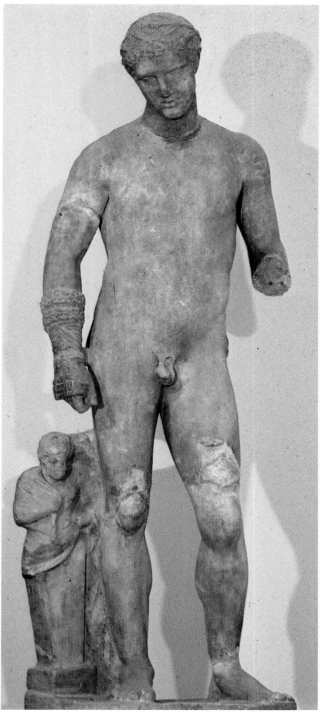

Statue of the Lance Bearer, marble, 2.11 m, prov. Pompeii, Samnite Palaestra

Statue of the Wrestler (Palestrita), Greek marble, height 1.68 m, prov. Sorrento, Palaestra

itself, but subordinating the expression of sentiment to pure formal beauty.

Orestes and Electra

Statuary group probably coming from the School of Praxiteles operating in Rome between the end of the Republic and the beginning of the Empire.

In some elements it recalls eclectically the Severe Period (480-450 B.C.) in others the Hellenistic one.

Diomedes of Kresilas, copy of an original of the V Cent. B.C., marble, 1.77 m, prov. Cumae

Orestes and Electra, marble, height 1.50 m, prov. Pozzuoli, Public Market erroneously known as Temple of Serapis

Venus from Sinuessa

The fruit of a fortunate find near Mondragone, the ancient Sinuessa which gave her the name, is a beautiful statue of a naked woman, made in Greek marble, an Hellenistic original which could be placed in the II Cent. B.C. Since the head and the arms are missing, reconstruction of the attitudes, based on comparisons, suggests that it may be of Venus who, leaving the sea, brings her hands to her head to arrange her hair, while her mantle slides down to her legs revealing her beautiful form. The weight of the body, carried on the right leg, while the left one slightly bent forward, comes closer to the other to stop the mantle falling still further down, compels the goddess to move to the left to avoid losing her balance. This was a useful pretext for the sculptor to round off the shape and emphasize, with plastic softness, a body which, born to celebrate the beauty of the divine figure of the goddess, ends by suggesting a warm and morbid sensuality with the complicity of the colour of the Parian marble and the lighting effects pointing out the contrast between the naked body, on which the light settles sweetly, and the impenetrable pleats of the mantle.

Venus from Sinuessa, Greek marble, height 1.82 m.

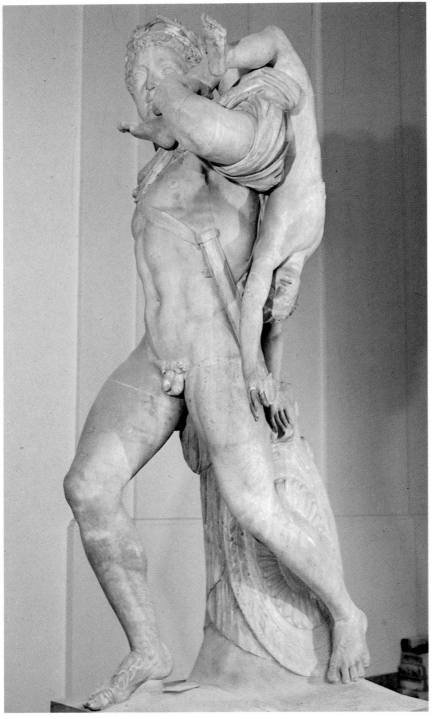

Hero with corpse of young boy (Hector or Troilus?), marble 2.87 m, prov. Farnese Collection, Rome, Caracalla Thermae

Hector and Troilus

Another marble group comes from the Thermae of Caracalla; it represents a naked man who seems to advance quickly, with the right leg stretched forward, to throw away an object or even to protect it. Although his figure is strong, it is also agile and elegant, being supported by a trunk covered with a cloth. The hero has the features of the Emperor Commodus, owing to a restoration by Calí, who, in addition to the head, may also have restored the right arm and changed its position. Hector carries on his back the dead body of a boy which he holds with his left hand, while the right, now unarmed, probably held a sword, the empty sheath of which hangs over his left shoulder. On the interpretation of the hero's attitude, i. e. of boldness or brave pity, depends the interpretation of the group which appears to some, to be Neoptolemus, son of Achilles, at the moment of throwing from a tower of Troy Astyanaxy, son of Hector and Andromache. In fact the attitude towards the body of the boy seems that irreverently reserved for a vanquished enemy. However to me it seems better to attribute that position to the passion and tragedy of the moment, and see in the group, Hector bringing to safety the corpse of Troilus, the youngest of Priam's sons, killed by Achilles near the altar of Apollo Timbreus. This could also explain the original idea of the right hand grasping the sword to defend the body from further violence. Based on similar groups (Menelaus and Patroclus, Ulysses and Diomedes), this copy of Imperial Roman age seems to refer to an indeterminate Hellenistic original.

The Farnese Flora, Greek marble, height 3.42 m.

The Farnese Flora

This is the colossal statue after which the Gallery housing it is named and which, after many restorations, at first by Guglielmo Della Porta (end of the XVI Cent.) then, about two centuries later, by Carlo Albacini and Filippo Tagliolini, - was the subject of greatly differing hypotheses, since its attributes (especially the bunch of flowers) were not considered original by anyone. Thus some saw an analogy with the Aphrodite of Cos by Praxiteles or a dance Muse, others an Hebe, near the Farnese Hercules, putting not flowers, but a cup or similar object in his hand in order to be able to offer a drink to the hero, at the moment of his entry into Olympus. In its present state, however, it represents the personification of Spring: a young woman whose beautiful figure can be seen through the very light chiton, which she holds up with her right hand to allow her to walk in comfort. She advances with elegance towards a precise place where she looks with eyes, emphasized by the short curly hair gathered at the back, putting her weight on the right leg, while the left, in movement, allows the transparent chiton to fold closely around her body. In spite of the colossal proportions, the statue maintains a certain elegance and nobility of bearing in the forms and movements. As already mentioned, it is with considerable grace that the woman holds up the chiton with her right hand and offers the bunch of flowers with her left. All this makes us think of another original of the IV Cent. B.C., which may be attributed to an artist of the Praxiteles school. In this Roman copy there may be found stylistic characteristics of the II-III Cent. A.D. and motifs later taken as examples in various representations of Victories in following ages.

Venus Callipige

From the Domus Aurea of Nero, before ending in the Farnese Collection, comes an excellent Roman copy of an Hellenistic original, representing Aphrodite half-naked and known as Venus Callipige (Kallipygos = with beautiful nates), wrongly applied to another similar divinity sheltered - according to Athenaeus - in a temple in Syracuse and which could not be justified in a place of workship for its sensuality. The goddess who, in fact, has a very youthful appearance, is represented while uncovering her body by lifting the light, thickly pleated and belted chiton with her arms; pleased with her own figure, she turns to admire her reflection in the water in which she is probably about to bath. The statue would seem in fact to be destined for the middle of a small lake, so that, imagining her in such an ambience, the excessive sensuality and very feminine affectation issuing from her body would certainly be attenuated. The body is elegantly shaped as a spiral and made to be looked at from all sides, almost the mistress of the space surrounding her, with as accomplice a subtle light and shade effect, created by a contrast of diffused and elusive light on the bare skin and the stillness in the shadows of the crisp hair and of the chiton pleats.

This is the phase in which (between the III and II Cent. B.C.) Hellenistic art, ranging over an infinity of subjects and themes treated in a variety of ways, produced an infinity of results which, not always valid, were nevertheless useful to the breaking up of certain outlines and to the exigencies of taste and the changing life of the time.

Venus Callipige, marble, height 1.52 m, prov. Farnese Collection

Farnese Hercules

This mighty statue of Hercules, about m. 3 high, also from the Caracalla Thermae, as is the group of the "Bull" in front of which it is placed, perhaps represents the hero at the height of his labours. This statue, to which (1796) the legs had been added by Tagliolini on a model by Michelangelo before the right ones had been found and replaced, has the signature of a Greek artist, Gliconus, who evidently received an order for it during the Imperial age from some rich Roman, in the fervour for imitations of the Greek masterpieces.

In fact, one of these latter, probably the bronze statue by Lisippus, the great sculptor of Sicione, served as the prototype for numerous copies, all more or less different from the original, which however it is not difficult to trace back to, thanks above all, to a small Umbrian bronze at present in the Museum of the Louvre. The hero, who in ancient times was usually portrayed in movement, that is to say, while at his labours, had already by the V Cent. B.C. begun to be portrayed as a figure in repose with the club on the shoulder and the body resting on one leg, to which the other, lightly bent, gave balance. With the passing of the centuries this attitude of repose became one of complete abandonment so that, in the case of the Naples copy, to physical exhaustion was added an authentic moral depression. With the body lying abandoned, the club, covered with lion skin, acting as a support under the left arm pit, and on which the now bare arm rests; the left leg carrying the weight and placed slightly forward to balance the right arm which is behind the back holding the Golden Apples of the Hesperides, the bearded and microcephalous hero appears to be worn out by his great enterprises and sad at the approach of his passing to Olympus, in spite of the fact that triumph and eternal youth await him. It seems that the artist, ignoring the model, has intentionally emphasized the contrast between the lost physical strength and an inevitable destiny, ending by instilling in us a sense of human fragility.

Farnese Hercules, marble 3.17 m, prov. Farnese Collection, Rome, Caracalla Thermae

Group of the Farnese Bull, marble 3.70 m, prov. Farnese Collection, Rome, Caracalla Thermae

The Farnese Bull

This is the mythical story of the torture of Dirce, tied up to a bull by her step-sons Ampheon and Zethus, sons of Lycus, king of Thebes, who wanted to revenge their mother Antiope, who had been tied up and abandoned on Mount Cithaeron when she was pregnant with them, to leave their father free for his new love.

The group in the Naples Museum is a copy of Roman age from the Caracalla Thermae, changed and restored several times, mainly in the heads and arms. Restorations suggested by Michelangelo but badly executed by Biondi first and by Calí later, added to figures not present in the original, certainly altered its real image. From Pliny in fact we learn that the tragic theme, dear to Hellenistic sculpture for the exasperation of the feelings, had already been used by Apollonius and Tauriscus of Tralles in a bronze work, bought later in Greece by Asinius Pollion. This work would have been simpler and more linear, and its pyramidal scheme clearer, since it was placed on a triangular base and without the figures of Antiope on the back or of Mount Cithaeron, personified by a young boy with long hair, watching between impassivity and astonishment. Nevertheless the animated scene, thanks to the interrelation of the bodies and gestures of the four main figures, has not completely lost the pathos of a tragic event, increased by the imploring look of Dirce who vainly tries to free herself from the fore legs of the bull, kept high, and from a barking dog, which increases the confusion of the last moment, before the unhappy woman is dragged down the mountain.

Ephesian Artemis

Realized in precious alabaster, with bronze for the face, hands and feet, this is a tall statue dedicated in the Hadrian age to Ephesian Artemis, the goddess ruling Nature and wild animals, she who nourishes all living beings.

Covered from head to foot as it is by symbols, this statue takes us back immediately to the Oriental veneration of Artemis of Ephesus. Above an Ionic chiton falling to her feet, her cylindrical body is enclosed in an armoured garment divided into panels decorated with wild animals and at the waist with a protruding decoration of many breasts. These increase her femininity as mother dispenser of vital lymph for human and non human beings whom she dominates and nourishes and who cling to her everywhere, and to her arms and the disc like a halo protecting her head with the turreted crown. This also is a royal symbol just as the signs of the zodiac and the four winged maidens on the shield edged with festoons of hanging acorns, which covers her breast, are symbols of the seasons. The delicacy of the execution is also underlined by the colourful contrast between the warm tones of the alabaster and the black bronze, a contrast reminding us of that of certain black Madonnas dressed in precious materials embroidered in gold. And like this latter, also the Ephesian Artemis has her arms open ready to receive in her lap anyone needing to drink at her source.

Among all the copies of the original which exists in Ephesus, due to the diffusion of the veneration of this idol from the East to Rome, through Ionia and Greece, this one in Naples remains the best, since it conserves the schematic shape of the original, which has been lost on the other hand in the more modern style of the head and of the naturalistic elements.

Ephesian Artemis, alabaster and bronze, height 2.03 m, prov. Farnese Collection

Apollo Citharist

Also this statue, like the Ephesian Artemis probably had arms, hands and feet in bronze, those parts which were found to be missing and which were added later in white marble by Albacini, who restored it and gave it the appearance of Apollo. The "laureate" god sits on a rock with the left leg slightly forward. He holds the lyre with the left hand and with the right resting on the knee, clasps the plectrum. Evidently the god is showing off his divine singing and playing.

He is, in fact, dressed in theatrical costume, i. e. with the talaric tunic with tight sleeves and belt around the breast instead of the waist; he wears over it a mantle buckled on the shoulders and folded on the right knee. Because the original head is missing, we cannot say anything about the expression of the god's face, even if the restorations seem right according to the types reproduced on a coin of Beozia and on a relief in Cyprus, which indicate as model an original of the IV Cent. B.C. The red porphyry used in the original parts certainly helps to add value to the accuracy of the execution.

Apollo Citharist, red porphyry and white marble, height 1.82 m, prov. Farnese Collection

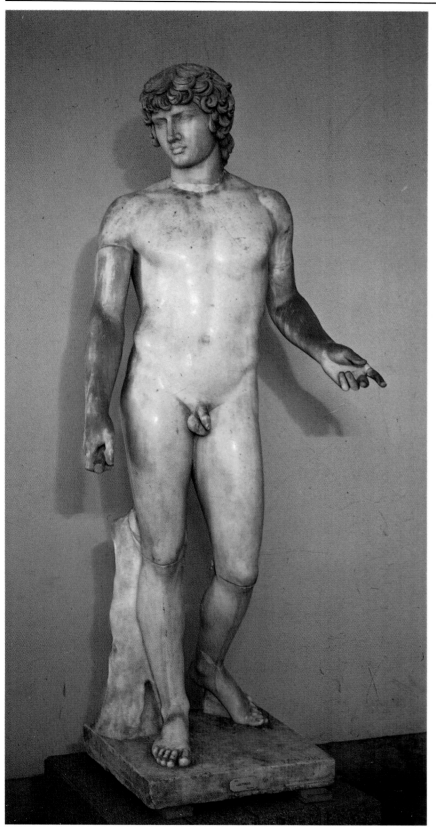

Antinous

A real artistic fervour was caused in the Hadrian age by the beautiful figure of the young boy Antinous who arrived as a slave from Bythinia and entered so much into the emperor Hadrian's graces as to become his favourite. Drowned in the Nile in mysterious circumstances (propitiatory self-sacrifice or eventual jealousies?) while going up the river with the imperial court retinue in 10 A.D.; he was bitterly lamented by the desperate emperor who conferred on him divine honours and had him portrayed looking like Dionysus and Adonis.

This statue in the Naples Museum, from the Farnese Collection, represents him with his human features but with attitudes full of grace, accentuated by a body accurately refined. The ephebic beauty comes mainly from the oval face, slightly inclined forwards and framed by the curly hair covering his forehead. From the deepset eyes spreads the languid and sad beauty which fascinated the emperor.

Antinous, marble 2.00 m, prov. Farnese Collection

Greek Portraiture

The religious concept according to which only the gods, to whose level it was not possible to rise without risking an accusation of boasting (ubris), could be portrayed, certainly delayed the development of the art of portraiture in Greece. The votive character of the archaic portrait also contributed to this delay, since it was used more to ingratiate oneself with the god in whose temple it was dedicated, than to create an image resembling the model. Thus, at least at the beginning, the Greek portrait had to be lacking in any characterisation, and aim at seeing the subject, according to the case, as the ideal of his particular type - warrior, athlete, or man of letters, etc. This fact led, in the V Cent. B.C., to the portrayal, without any distinction between them, of both gods and heroes, in the frieze of the Parthenon. But in the following Century, i.e. when with the decline of Athenian imperialism it was preferred to represent poets and philosophers instead of army leaders, things had to be changed considerably, even if they resorted to oral and literary sources to "reconstruct" otherwise unknown features, or even resort to true and proper invention as, according to Pliny, happened later also in the Roman sphere, when absolutely no indication or information regarding their personalities, was available to the portraitist of illustrious men. But it seems that not even Pliny himself could complain about this fact, since he criticized the excessive realism of certain portraits and praised Cresila for having ennobled men. Nevertheless, as already mentioned, the tendency to individualism, triumphing in Greek thought in the IV Cent. B.C., influenced art and particularly portraiture. And it was in fact in this ambience that the, by no means incredible, word was spread that Lysitratos, brother of Lisippus, in order to obtain faithful portraits, made masks from life.

Portrait of Euripides, marble, Roman copy, 0.61 m, prov. Farnese Collection

Portrait of Socrates, marble, Roman copy, 0.94 m, prov. Farnese Collection

Portrait of Homer, marble, Roman copy, 0.51 m, prov. Farnese Collection

Roman Portraiture

Also Roman portraiture like the Greek, has a religious origin, since the ancient Romans started to make mortuary masks (the images kept in the "armaria" of the atria of the houses) which owing to their nature immediately arrived at "realism". From them, thanks to the mediation of the Chiusine canopi, it was an easy step to the bust, which in sepulchral monuments was enclosed in an aedicule and sometimes in a circular frame. But this kind of macabre realism was changed by naturalistic trends of Italic origin, which asserted themselves in Roman art from the II Cent. B.C. and later also by Greek trends. It was with the fusion of these three trends, Italic, Roman and Greek, that was realized the conception of Roman portraiture which aimed, in the Imperial age, at exalting to the maximum the prince's own features, rather than raising him, as happened in Greece for Alexander, to divine rank. And as happened in Greece for that king, so did it happen in Rome for the descendants of Augustus who wanted their portraits made to his model, but without losing their own individual characteristics. Of course private portraits enjoyed greater freedom as clearly shown by the Pompeian portraits of the actor Norbanus Sorex, of Tiberian age, and of the banker Caecilius Jucundus, of Neronian age.

Portrait of Julius Caecilius Jucundus, bronze, 0.35 m, prov. Pompeii, House of J.C. Jucundus

Portrait of Norbanus Sorex, bronze, 0.355 m, from Pompeii, Temple of Isis, Room LXXII.

1) *Funerary steles with scenes of offerings*
2) *Necklaces in coloured glass paste*
3) *A mummy in glass case*
4) *Wooden case for funeral statuettes*

Egyptian Art

Certainly this is not the right place to talk profusely about Egyptian art, in some ways the most ancient in the world, about which everybody knows the great production, its language and writing, its religion, about which much information has been lost and many still try to rediscover from the Bible and the Greek and Roman writers and above all by direct observation of what remains to us and what is still being produced by the excavations, thanks also to the now decoded mysteries of the hieroglyphic signs of its writing. Of course all the artistic or pseudo-artistic manifestations connected with the life of this population, talk to us more or less clearly about the various periods of its history, about the great dynasties of its Pharaohs, builders of great pyramids (Cheops, Chefrem and Mycerinus), about foreign domination such as the Assyrian, the Persian and so on until the Greek, the Roman and the Arabian. But a particular study should be directed to the religion of this people, since thanks to it, directly or not, precious evidence of this civilization has reached us. In fact Egypt, in addition to the great monuments, has bequeathed to posterity a large number of objects, devotionary statuettes, utensils of the cult, funerary furniture. And these last especially constitute the patrimony of our museums, sometimes as wall fragments of sepulchral rooms, funeral steles, painted chests, funeral vases and statuettes, mummies and also papyri with formularies and prayers necessary to the dead to purify their souls before mingling with the divine. The walls and the doors of the funeral chambers, often majestic, have engraved on them figures of dead and of divinities which are explained in long writings with names of kings and of dignitaries, with texts of prayers which we find repeated also on funeral steles, where ritual scenes and scenes of sacred offerings are more frequent. The stone sarcophagi sometimes similar to houses contained wooden chests decorated with funeral subjects in which the mummies were conserved, tightly wrapped in bandages which protected and preserved the body, for as long as possible because the soul returned to it from time to time to undergo punishments until total purification. And on those bandages there were placed also devotionary objects and amulets alluding to the resurrection, to the divine power, to the prize reserved to the just. Near the funeral chest were placed also vases shaped with human or animal heads, known as Canopi or Canopic vases because the head recalled the god Canopus; inside them the entrails of the embalmed bodies were placed. The inscriptions on these vases invoked the protection of the infernal divinities just as the papyri of the tombs contain texts of poems, stories, treatises about morals or medicine, but more frequently prayers for the dead, often illustrated with coloured sketches alluding to the soul's voyage to the hereafter, and the funeral liturgies used when the corpse left the house and, after long ceremonies, reached the tomb in the necropolis. And these were easily recognizable for a kind of architecture particularly rich in motives in the form of lotus flowers, hieroglyphics, the figures of Pharaohs. This was an art which immediately struck the fantasy of Greeks and Romans, who copied it and borrowed religious ideas from it.

Mosaics

Not unlike painting, of which the mosaic art is a direct "daughter" as to subjects and colours and from which it differs only in the procedure, the Naples Museum keeps some noteworthy examples of this art which, born during the late Classicism and developed in the Hellenistic Roman ambience, found its main centre of production in Alexandria in Egypt, from where it arrived in Italy, and consequently underwent further development and new techniques of application.

To satisfy particular tastes and exigences there were still the three classical types of work: the tesselated, the vermiculated and the inlay or "opus sectile". The first using small marble cubes almost always white or black, were suitable mainly for geometrical designs or lines for setting and framing other motives. The second, of finest manufacture because the marble or coloured glass cubes were very small and suitable mainly for figured compositions made in squares of limited sizes, on wood, terracotta or travertine (emblemata) bases, was carried out directly in the workshop of a craftsman, for insertion into large compositions. The third type, also used preferably for geometrical motives, consisted in cutting the material, not into cubes, but into shapes or parts of designs which were set into the empty spaces of a plane realized in a different way, thus creating a type of inlay work.

For mosaics of large dimensions for decorating whole floors, walls, columns or basins of fountains, the work had obviously to be done in situ, after the preparation of the base for application of the tesserae and with the cooperation of workmen skilled in cutting, drawing or installation.

Doves drinking from a basin, mosaic, prov. Pompeii 1.13 x 1.13 m.

Cupid riding a lion, mosaic, 1.63 x 1.63 m, prov. Pompeii, House of the Faun

The Battle of Alexander

Battle of Alexander against Darius, mosaic, h. 3.42 x 5.92 m, prov. Pompeii, House of the Faun

An animated scene of war is the subject of a great mosaic from the House of the Faun in ancient Pompeii, the same house from which came the "Cat biting a Partridge" and the "Winged Genius on a Panther". It was a floor in an exedra and was made when the house, of Samnite origin, had long been in the possession of a Roman who transformed it according to the prevailing taste for Hellenistic art. The great mosaic work could be dated in the last years of Pompeii, if the original Greek painting it reproduces is in fact the one hung in the Temple of Peace dedicated in Rome in 75 A.D. However, the problem of the pictorial origin, according to available sources, is not of easy solution, even if we are inclined to see it as the work of Philossenus, student of Timomacus, and probable author of a painting representing a famous battle between Darius and Alexander (that of Isso in Cilicia of 333 B.C.?) like the mosaic in question. The "opus vermiculatum" technique used, makes it appear as a grandiose symbol, over the execution of which there almost certainly presided Alexandrine artists, whose hand is even easier to

recognize in the other mosaics of the house mentioned, which, using very small tesserae could solve any problem of continuity of line and shading of colour brilliantly, in spite of having used for the latter only four foundamental tones: white, yellow, red and black. Just this trick, together with the wise distribution of the masses blended with a surprising abundance of details where the eye cannot lose itself in empty spaces, makes of it a masterpiece of unity. Although there is no landscape in the background, apart from a bare and stylized tree, the composition does not appear flat thanks to the bold foreshortenings necessary to illustrate the confusion of bodies, human and non-human, and of all the destruction. But the attention is drawn directly by the fray and the two protagonists: on the left Alexander, with head uncovered among the pressing Macedonian army; on the right Darius calling, in vain, on the retreating Persians. With this beautiful work the artist surely wrote a wonderful page of history.

Dionysiac Scenes

Undoubtedly Dionysus is entitled to one of the places of honour among the divinities of ancient Greece. He represented the vegetable life of Nature and it was he who found the vine and gave it to everybody, becoming the god of wine and inebriation. Ivy crowned and followed by a cheerful group (the thiasos) of Nymphs, Satyrs and other Genii of the wood, he made the mountains resound with uproar and wild foolishness, giving joy and oblivion to others and becoming himself, according to different myths, persecuted, tormented and killed. So that the double nature, merry and sad, gave origin, for everyone who adored him, to two distinct rites. The simpler ones were celebrated In Spring and Autumn (during the vintage), the others, more complicated and full of meaning, every two years during the Winter solstice. These last were orgiastic and mystic feasts which were held among inaccessible woods by women (Menads or Bacchantes) who, being prey to mystical ecstasies, abandoned themselves to whirling dances and foolish gestures shouting and carrying torches and thyrsi (twisted sticks of ivy and wine-leaves surmounted by a pine-cone) in noisy nocturnal processions. Several objects from the Archaeological Excavations of the Vesuvian towns refer to this orgiastic cult as in fact the two scenes mentioned. In these, on a black background recalling the wild nights, some initiates (this was the name given to those belonging secretly to the cult) are abandoning themselves to the mystic euphoria shaking sacred vestments. In fact different attributes are recognizable, cups of various shapes to drink the wine, torches to light up the night, holy bands, Thyrsi, fawn skins (the nebris with which the Bacchantes covered themselves), the phallus (symbol of

Bacchic Rite, sectile work. Prov. Pompeii 0.21 x 0.67 m.

Maenad and Satyr, sectile work. Prov. Pompeii 0.23 x 0.67 m.

the productive force of Nature) and sacred images of the divinities, such as Priapus, often companion of Dionysus, and a panther which advances looking backwards, i.e. one of the animals (donkey, goat, bull) which are sacred to god Dionysus.

Cocks Fighting, mosaic, 0.53 x 0.54 m, prov. Pompeii

Panther with Dionysiac symbols, mosaic, prov. Pompeii 0.110 x 0.110 m.

Head of a Gorgon, mosaic, prov. Pompeii 0.12 x 0.89 m.

The Graces, mosaic, prov. Pompeii
0.98 x 0.87 m

The Graces

Among the subjects often repeated in sculpture, painting and mosaic, are the three Graces, all copies of the same original, portraying the side ones from the front, and the centre one from the back.

They are usually shown wearing crowns of small leaves and flowers, and holding bunches of the same in their free hands, while the figure in the centre usually holds an apple in her right hand.

The mosaic reproduced here differs in various respects and has lost much due to the bad state of preservation. The figures must however have stood out well on a background which has been destroyed, although the design and the execution are rather rough, also because of the material used, since of course the large tesserae were not suitable for works of small dimensions, richness of detail or graduated colours.

Frieze with festoons and masks. Pompeiian mosaic: House of the Faun

Marine Fauna, mosaic, 0.118 x 0.118 m, prov. Pompeii, House of the Faun

Academy of Plato, mosaic, 0.85 x 0.85 m, prov. Pompeii, Suburb

Academy of Plato

From a Villa near Pompeii comes a beautiful mosaic of Roman age and historical subject which, with its square frame decorated with festoons of theatrical masks, flowers, and fruit, recalls those at the House of the Faun.

Magic Consultation, mosaic, 0.45 x 0.365 m, prov. Pompeii, Villa of Cicero

Magic Consultation and Itinerant Musicians

Two mosaic works regularly "signed" ("Dioskourides Samios epoiese" = Dioscurides of Samo made it) may be defined as real master's paintings. They come from the so-called Villa of Cicero in Pompeii. This is one of the few cases in which we find the name of the artist on works which have come from the town covered by the Vesuvian eruption of 79 A.D. In the two mosaics made between the II and the I Cent. B.C. the author reveals, even before the technical mastery and taste of his execution, a real freshness of inspiration certainly nourished by real and direct observation of scenes of

Itinerant Musicians, mosaic, 0.48 x 0.46 m, prov. Pompeii, Villa of Cicero

every-day life which had become part of the repertory of the comic theatre. Nevertheless the brilliant results obtained by the liveliness of the colours used, have, unfortunately, been spoiled, at least in the first picture (Magic Consultation) by a rigid schematism with horizontal and vertical stripes which detract from the real function of the frame, expanding until they fill the background to the figures, which are still further flattened by the monochrome wall without objects in the background. In the other scene (Itinerant Musicians), on the contrary, even if the artist has used a similar expedient for framing the figures, this time in a less

rigid way, the lively movement of the same and of their shadows, which was possible also thanks to the different environment - this time the street - occupied by the figures, the rigid schematism seems and indeed is literally broken up, resulting in a more highly artistic production.

1) The Magic consultation is depicted with humorous theatrical effects, where two women sitting on a triclinium watch a sorceress intent on preparing for them a magic filter, on which she angrily invokes the infernal forces to give it the requested power. The witch gazes fixedly into the distance as if she had already seen the approach of the evil power, while her two customers, half attentive half terrorized recite the ritual together with her. The comical masks of

the faces tell us that it is really only a farce.

2) The other picture, the Itinerant Musicians, with the four people wandering in the streets, is also of theatrical inspiration. The gaiety of the musicians, produced with the songs and sounds of their performance, is even more than doubled by the clumsiness with which they move, intent as they are on following the rhythm of their instruments: timbal, tambourine and flute. The lively street scene is completed by a boy looking more like a dwarf, one of those figures who, joining the touring companies, cause great hilarity without doing anything at all. There still emanates from the masked faces the rich and afflicted spiritually of those who sell fun only for a job.

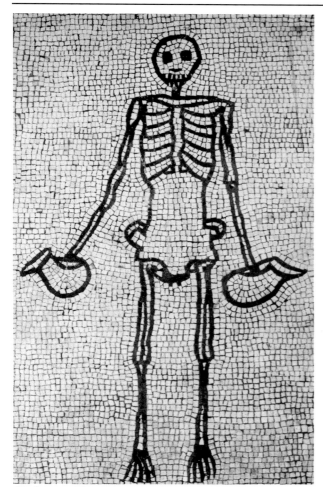

Skeleton with pitchers (mosaic).
Subject inspired by Epicurean philosophy

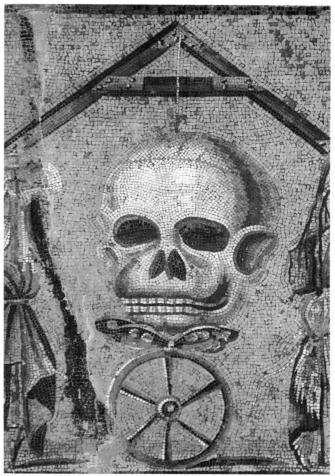

Skull with the symbols of life and death, mosaic found in Pompeii

To this impression undoubtedly contribute the warm tones of the colours used, which with light and shadow effects and with the movement given to the figures, put this work before the other, which is colder and less rich in humanity.

The Dancing Faun. Bronze, h. 0.71 m. Prov. Pompeii, House of the Faun
Pompeiian mosaic dating from before 79 A.D. Portrait of a woman, prov. Pompeii

The Dancing Faun

From one of the most beautiful of the Samnite Houses of Pompeii, that gave us back wonder-ful masterpieces of mosaic art (such as the famous Battle of Alexander, the Winged Genius on a Panther, Cupid riding a lion, and others) comes an admirable bronze representing a Satyr dancing or in prey of a Dionysiac orgy.

It adorned the impluvium of a house which was named after it and which was brought to light in 1830.

This valuable work, an original datable between the III and the II Cent. B.C., came down to us in a good state of preservation, and is an excellent example of how Hellenistic art had changed the themes of the ancient art and invented new and bold schemes.

The statuette in question in fact depicts the God of the Woods while abandoned to a whirling and jumping dance.

He has just sprung up onto his toes and a quiver, rippling through his limbs seems to involve all the space around him, which he dominates with an upward glance and with arms raised in time to the music which he accompanies with the dance and the snapping of his fingers.

No part of his body is still, because the euphoric excitement has spread to the very top of his beard and his tousled hair, and issues from his whole body, including the silvery eyes.

It is a kind of celebration of the merry life that he lives in the woods and on the mountains, along with a touch of orgiastic abandonment to Bacchic ecstasy.

There is great harmony in the separate parts and the plastic softness of the chiaroscuro play of the light which, while spreading smoothly over his entirely nude body, is sometimes boldly interrupted by his unforeseeable gestures.

The Pictorial Collection

As to ancient painting, the National Archaeological Museum of Naples must be considered a true and proper picture gallery, because apart from the few funerary paintings from tombs of Isernia, Ruvo, Egnazia, Paestum and Cumae, it has several pieces of civil painting which adorned public and private buildings in the towns covered by the famous Vesuvian eruption of 79 B.C. The first, even if only few in number, give us an idea of the lively pictorial decoration carried out on walls of Italic chamber tombs, constituting, also for its documentary character, a valuable testimony to pre-Roman customs and ethnic types, especially the Osco-Samnites of Campania. For their artistic characteristics these paintings constitute a reflection of Greek and Etruscan painting of the V and IV Cent. B.C. Because of the lack of any background landscape these scenes have, indipendently of their dimensions, a certain air of solemnity outside normal space and time and therefore particularly in harmony with the sepulchral ambience. This impression is increased by the strong and lively tones of the colours used which, making the figures stand out from the ivory-white background with which they contrast, underline their gestures which, sometimes repeated as in the Funeral Choir of Ruvo (p.44), assume a dignified composure far from any suggestion of monotony.

As to the paintings from the Vesuvian towns the discourse is different, because for an exact understanding of them, it would be necessary to have at least some knowledge of the Archaeological Excavations of Pompeii, Herculaneum and Stabiae, to which they belonged. This is not necessary, at least for those subjects executed outside those places and subsequently added to a larger pictorial composition. With regard to the technique of execution, most of them are frescoes carried out on a carefully prepared background, although there are some works, perhaps only retouchings, done with tempera. The colours were mixed with marble powder, which made them particularly compact, while a protective coat of wax gave them a special brightness. This kind of painting developed around the I Cent. A.D. and knew various phases divided for convenience of study into 4 styles: the first, rather than true painting, was stucco decoration; the second was distinguished for a research into space; the third for a geometrical schematization; the fourth for exuberant and Baroque decoration.

So that inside large compositions conceived in this way and occupying entire walls, they inserted square-panels of limited dimensions, sometimes made elsewhere, the theme of which was often taken from Greek mythology but with such an abundance that it shows how large was the repertory of Greek models and of originals which these craftsmen kept in sight, even if using already prepared cartoons. In fact we cannot talk, except in a few cases, of real artists, since most of them were good Italiot craftsmen , working in the area of Campania already Romanized and under the influence of the Greek Neapolis. However, although strictly depending on the Greek style, because of the technical and spiritual work of the local craftsmen, this painting acquired a character of its own, thus allowing us to talk about Roman- Campanian art; in fact the Greek myth

Love Punished, fresco 1.54 x 1.16 m. Prov. Pompeii.

Samnite warriors and knights, tomb painting of the IV Cent. B.C., 1.12 x 1.99 m. Prov. Paestum

Departure scene, tomb painting of the IV Cent. B.C., 1.15 x 2.10 m. Prov. Paestum.

46

Painted Wall, architecture with door and masks, fresco in II style. Prov. Boscoreale : Villa of P. FANNIUS SYNISTOR, triclinium 3.37 x 1.2 m.

was re-interpreted adding Italic and Roman elements. There were however few cases in which these figures were not treated in square-panels but in continuous friezes and of natural size. Of these megalographic arts the Museum of Naples contains in part the one from a Villa of Boscoreale, representing an historical scene of doubtful interpretation, while another more famous one, the subject of which seems to allude to the Dionysiac Mysteries, remained in its place in the Pompeian Villa called "of the Mysteries". To complete the picture of this painting there is no shortage of scenes of municipal life and customs, which, although classified as minor types, show by their documentary importance that they do not merit such a name. Also the portrait, the landscape, and the still-life met the favour of purchasers with different preferences, but it is better to refer to these separately in this work, when commenting on specific objects.

Here finally we cannot but remember the essential function which the Neapolitan Pictorial Collection has as an insubstitutable means of obtaining knowledge of Greek painting of which unfortunately so little remains to us.

Painted Wall, theatrical scenery, fresco in IV style, 1.98 x 1.32 m. Prov. Herculaneum.

Hercules and Telephus, fresco, 2.02 x 1.71 m, prov. Herculaneum, Basilica, IV style

The Love of Mars and Venus, fresco 2.53 x 1.50 m, prov. Pompeii : House of the Citharist

Hercules and Telephus

The glorification of the Attalids of Pergamum is the theme of a great painting from the Herculaneum Basilica and reproducing the myth of Telephus, unnatural son of Hercules and Auge, exposed on mount Partheneus so that the girl-mother could not kill him and where he was nourished by a fawn, until he became the founder of the royal family. The action of the figures is caught at the culminating moment, when Hercules, on indication by the winged Nemesis behind him, recognizes his little son under the doe holding him by the waist and sweetly licking his knee with its tongue. At the centre sitting majestically on a rock, the head crowned with vine leaves, a knobbly sceptre in the left hand, the thoughtful eyes lost among the mountains, is the personification of Arcadia, the land of myth. Behind her a smiling little satyr interrupts the playing of his syrinx to enjoy the idillic scene, completed with a basket of grapes and lower down, between the feet of the woman and the hero, an eagle and a lion, symbols of royal power. The myth which has nothing original in itself, does not prevent the painting having its rightful place among the most celebrated Campanian-Roman paintings reproducing Hellenistic originals, in this case of the Pergamum School. The great complexity of the scene, well studied in the distribution of the figures, the majestic attitude of the same in the corposity of the volumes, frequently emphasized, as in the case of the doe, by very powerful foreshortenings, brings us to that matrix without detracting anything from from the ability of the Campanian artist who undoubtedly put a little autonomous Roman spirit into it. The fresco is therefore a mature work of an artist who in the fullness of the expressive means, works on an epic theme, giving it an almost monochrome intonation (ivory and brown) and humanizing it to obtain a joyful idyllic pastoral scene, likewise profused in the full basket of fruit with a note of fresh naturalism. A clever play of light and shade contributes with its alternation to completion of the rhythm of the composition.

Achilles and Chiron

The legendary wisdom of Chiron, a centaur completely different from the others for his gentleness which together with his intellectual qualities made him the mythical educator of heroes such as Actaeon, Aristeus, Hercules and others, is the theme of the great painting from the Herculaneum Basilica. This time the pupil of this exceptional teacher is a prodigious youth destined to legendary enterprises: Achilles, the fruit of a marriage favoured by Chiron himself through the wise advice given to Peleus to overcome the reluctance of Thetis.

Women playing with Astragals

Great fame was attached in antiquity to the Greek myth of Niobe, the daughter of the Lydian king Tantalus, who with her twelve children earned the envy of Leto, mother of Apollo and Artemis, who shared that hate and killed their twelve innocent rivals. Overcome by sorrow Niobe was turned into a stone and taken by the gods to mount Sypilus in Phrygia, where even in this state she continued to bemoan her misfortune. The allegorical meaning hidden in the myth is a little obscure, and consequently gets explained in different ways.

This is the theme of the present monochrome from Herculaneum, made with skillful ability in the very difficult art of encaustic painting on marble and executed at the beginning of the I Cent. A.D.

Achilles and Chiron, fresco, 1.24 x 1.18 m, prov. Herculaneum, Basilica, IV style

Women playing with astragals, encaustic painting on marble, 0.40 x 0.42 m, prov. Herculaneum, beginning of the I Cent. A.D.

51

Perseus and Andromeda

In Antiquity there was much celebration in artistic and literary works, of the myth of Andromeda, the innocent daughter of Cepheus and Cassiopea, king and queen of Ethiopia who, with their arrogance, had offended the Nereides, inhabitants of the sea. To avenge themselves the Nereides asked for help from their king, Poseidon, who, as punishment, sent a marine monster to Cepheus' beaches. To placate the divine anger and liberate the country from the monster, Cepheus was forced, as foreseen by an oracle, to sacrifice his daughter Andromeda. In this scene she is tied to a rock on the seashore awaiting extreme martyrdom when Perseus sees her from the sky where he is flying on the winged horse Pegasus, returning from a victorious battle with Medusa whose head he had cut off. He falls in love with the girl, kills the monster, frees Andromeda and marries her.

Perseus and Andomeda, fresco,
0.93 x 1.06 m, prov. Pompeii, House
of the Dioscuri, IV style

Medea killing her sons, fresco,
0.90 x 1.93 m, prov. Pompeii, House
of the Dioscuri, IV style

Medea killing her Sons

This is another part of the mythical story of Jason capturing the
Golden Fleece, for which undertaking the hero was helped by the
magic arts of Medea who subsequently became his wife in Iolcus.
But when they arrived in Corinth the hero fell in love with Glauce,
the daughter of the king Creon, and tried unsuccessful to persuade
Medea to annul their marriage amicably; but she revenged herself
by causing her rival to be burnt to death and killing her own and
Jason's sons.

Theseus and the Minotaur

The noted myth of Theseus who, with the help of Ariadne who was in love with him, succeeded in killing the Minotaur, a monster with a human body and the head of a bull, to which the Athenians were forced to make a daily tribute of human flesh (boys and girls), finds in this painting from Pompeii, not so much an heroic glorification of the successful undertaking, as an expression of deeply felt gratitude and astonishment at the unimaginable liberation it represented for the people.

The Sacrifice of Iphigenia

In order to placate the anger of Artemis and allow the Greeks to continue their voyage towards Troy, it was necessary, according to the seer Calchas, for Agamemnon, king of Mycenae, who had offended the goddess by killing a sacred hart, to sacrifice his eldest daughter Iphigenia. The innocent girl was awaiting martyrdom when the goddess, taking pity on her, put a hart in her place and carried her to Tauris where she became the priestess of Artemis. This is the mythical theme of a Pompeian painting from the House of the Tragic Poet. It represents the girl already vowed to sacrifice being conducted to the altar by Ulysses and Diomede. Her white breast is already bared to receive the blow, because her dress of saffron, like those of the priestesses of Artemis, has fallen from her; and she opens her arms in a desperate appeal for pity. At the right of the group the seer, Calchas, stands majestic and thoughtful, having already forseen what was about to occur.

◀
Theseus and the Minotaur, fresco, 0.90 x 0.81 m, prov. Pompeii

The Sacrifice of Iphigenia, fresco, 1.23 x 1.26 m, prov. Pompeii, House of the Tragic Poet, IV style

The Spring, fresco, 0.39 x 0.31 m, prov. Stabiae: Villa of Ariadne

Huntress Diana

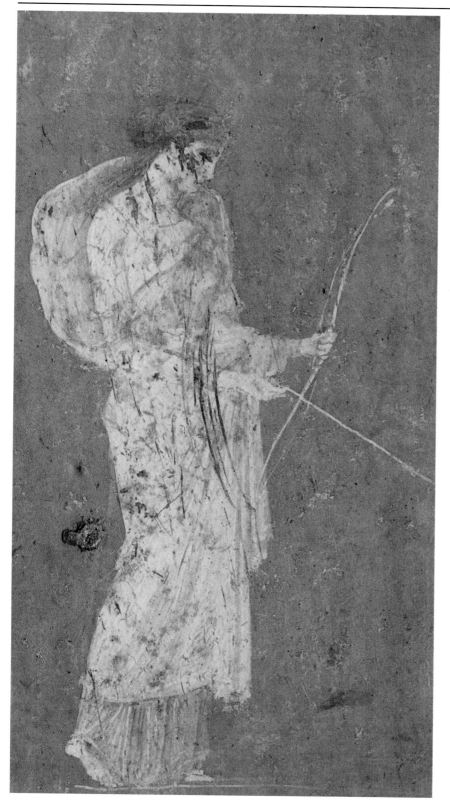

This is one of the four panels with feminine figures from the ancient excavations of Stabiae and it represents the huntress Artemis (Diana) while nocking an arrow on the bow she holds with the left hand. She is dressed in a long chiton just leaving her feet uncovered, advancing slowly and gracefully. On the sky-blue monochrome background the figure stands out also because the lack of a landscape background makes the attention fall entirely on the delicate feminine shape and on the refinement of the execution, also detracting from the subjects which I should call etheral, any corporeity to the advantage therefore of a symbolic abstraction.

The other three panels represent a woman with flowers (The Spring?) on a green background, Medea killing her sons on a sky-blue background and Leda with the swan also on a green background.

Huntress Diana, fresco, 0.39 x 0.31 m, prov. Stabiae: Villa of Ariadne

Landscape in Hellenistic-Campanian-Roman Painting

Although the landscape is still wrongly considered a "minor" theme in this type of painting, while on the contrary this kind undoubtedly tells us much more than certain large mythological compositions, since its Italic-Roman character - still showing itself from the artistic point of view an imitative art - contributes considerably to the knowledge of the environments, nearly always the towns recovered from the famous eruption of Vesuvius of 79 A.D., from which the landscape paintings come.

Already present in mythological compositions, where often it makes the background, a landscape achieves an importance of its own when it becomes the main theme, the human figure having assumed a secondary function in respect to naturalistic elements (woods, fields, rivers, marine views). Therefore certain very small human figures seem lost in majestic scenes of woods, sketched as they are with a few impressionistic lines, where also eventual architectonic elements are outlined with quick execution and lost in the vastness surrounding them.

Thus, from a comparison between vast and mysterious Nature and Man who loses himself in it there develops that sense of the arcane and the sacred, emphasized also by the presence of miniature temples or chapels that this painting has, in a type of landscape called sacro-idyllic, where the tones of the colours used give a greater or lesser freshness to the scene, regardless of whether the environment is in Italic, Roman or Egyptian style.

Idyllico-sacred Landscape, fresco 0.50 x 0.49 m. Prov. Pompeii

Seascapes, fresco 0.52 x 0.52 m. Prov. Stabiae

Paquius Proculus and his wife, fresco, 0.58 x 0.52 m. Prov. Pompeii: House of Paquius Proculus

Paquius Proculus and his Wife

Only the vanity of coarse, newly-rich persons can explain the execution of a portrait from Pompeii, depicting a couple indentified as Paquius Proculus, ex jurisdictionary duovir, and his wife, owners of the bakery (pistrinum) attached to the house where the painting was found.

The difficulty of attributing the painting to any effective citizens of the little Vesuvian town was due, obviously, to the features which characterize the two persons. There is no suggestion of idealization as there would be in the case of a purely decorative work. In fact the two bakers in question must have posed deliberately for a painter who, portraying them exactly as they wished, could do nothing to ennoble their features. They look like common working people who, personally, run a family business. The roll of papyrus that the man is holding below his chin in no way ennobles him nor does it present him as a Man of Letters, but suggests a merely conventional pose. The style of the woman holding waxed tablets in her hands, is better, she looks a good housewife and manager of her husband's business. Her hair, parted in front in the republican manner, which allows the odd impertinent curl to fall forwards, gives her rather more grace than her husband has. His hair is cut short and does no more than emphasize his bony features and the coarse details of his face. The warm tones of the colours used do contribute something to the characterization of the personalities, and with the richness of detail produced represent a masterpiece of Campano-Roman portraiture which certainly has a place among the most lifelike and realistic that the classical pictorial tradition has left to us.

Portrait of a Young Girl

The so-called "Sappho", one of the most noted portraits of Pompeian painting, depicts a young girl holding a stylus near her mouth with her right hand, while with the other she holds the waxed tablet on which she writes what she is thinking. She is in a thoughtful mood, with a distant glance concentrating on nothing. Her unruly curls held in place by a hairnet and her large round earrings give her a wholly feminine grace, to which contributes also the delicacy with which she holds the stylus and the tablet, which seem much more fitting in her case than in that of the commom companion of Paquius Proculus (see page 104). Nervertheless, the realistic features of the baker's wife contribute to the individualization of the personalities; an individualization which is difficult here, not so much for the conventional pose as for the idealization of the face which, perhaps for this very reason, seems a little cold. There is no plausible reason for seeing it as a portrait of the poetess of Lesbos.

Portrait of a young girl, fresco, diam. 0.29 m. Prov. Pompeii

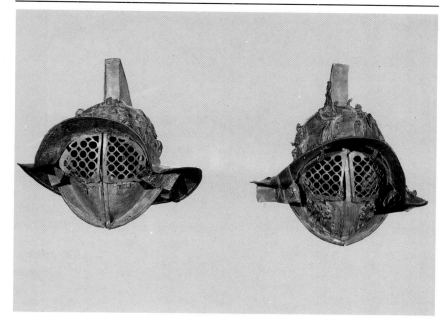

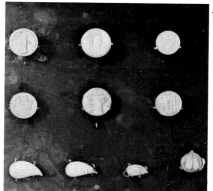

Gladiatorial Helmets

Rich and various are the proofs of the gladiatorial activity in the small Vesuvian towns covered by the eruption of 79 A.D.

Apart from the large buildings such as amphitheatres and palaestrae reserved for public shows and training, a considerable contribution to the documentation is represented by advertisements of shows, painted in large red characters on the walls of the houses, the several and more interesting graffiti concerning the subject, and also the weapons of various kinds used in the fights and found in the above mentioned buildings: short swords (the "glaudius" which named the relevant combats), jambs, curved lances, nets to restrain the adversary and helmets.

These latter unlike those used by the soldiers in the armies were more solid and more decorated with large edges to protect the nape of the neck, ears and forehead and with lattice visor to defend the eyes without precluding the sight. Often they became real masterpieces of local handicraft, so it is easy to imagine that they were also used for decoration and spectacle, in festive parades and in processions (pompae) which preceded the show of the true and proprer combats (munus).

In these cases, the artist, besides using simple embossed ornaments and isolated figures (often medusae, dolphins and other animals) also attempted complex scenes, made in high relief and taken from the epic repertory.

The helmets represented here come respectively from Pompeii and Herculaneum: on the first one is represented the Apotheosis of Rome, on the other the Iliupersis, i.e. the last night of Troy, with Cassandra taken violently away from Palladium by Ajax, the old Priam ill-treated by Neoptolemus, Aeneas escaping with old Anchises on his shoulders and Creusa unwilling to leave her son Ascanius.

1) Group portraying Perona and Mycon

2) Feminine toilet articles (brooches, combs)

3) Oil-lamps in various shapes

61

The Blue Vase

To the category of stained and engraved glass, almost all from the small towns covered by Vesuvius, belongs a beautiful cinerary urn found on the 29th December 1837 in a tomb of the necropolis of the Herculaneum Gate in Pompeii. It is certainly one of the most beautiful pieces of ancient glass work that have come down to us. It is a double glass amphora: the inner glass, coloured blue, is smooth and transparent; the outer one, white and opaque, is in inlay work with cameo technique. There are two themes treated in this last stratum: on the lower part, making a frieze are carved zoomorphic motives, on the upper part two scenes illustrate the grape harvest. In the middle of an intricate interlacing of vine-shoots still loaded with bunches of grapes, coming out from two big masks surrounded by ivy, are some Putti working and enjoying themselves. At one side one Putto shaking a thyrsus with the right hand is treading the grapes put by a friend into a basin, while two others, seated higher up are playing the double tibia and the syrinx. On the other side two Putti are picking grapes to the sound of a lyre played by a third friend, while a fourth Putto already inebriated by the juice of Bacchus rests on a couch sipping wine. The happy group must have been accompanied by the songs of birds hidden among the branches.

Thus an aura of fresh naturalism issues from the idyllic scene, captured with the immediacy of one who has absorbed directly the perfume of the countryside and enjoyed the work which between toil and sweat has become a joy.

With admirable artistic intuition and patience of a chiseller the unknown glass worker could not adapt to the round shapes of the vase any better motive than the natural curving and interlacing of a vine.

The Blue Vase, glass paste, height 0.30 m, diam. 0.15 m. Prov. Pompeii

Necklaces in glass paste

Beakers, goblets and jugs in coloured glass

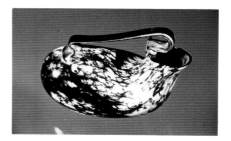

Table service, silver, 118 pieces, 24 kg. Prov. Pompeii, House of Menander

Silverware: a table service

This comes from the House of Menander in ancient Pompeii where it was found in December 1930 - a real treasure of silver ware. Owing to the restoration works being carried out in that house at the time of the eruption, the precious table service of the rich owner was kept wrapped up in woollen cloth in a wooden box placed in a room under the bathroom. This ensured the preservation until now, keeping the precious objects safe from plunderers (fossores) who visited the house just after the eruption. The table service consists of 118 pieces for a total weight of 24 kg among goblets and cups embossed and engraved, small cups, small bowls, basins, small jugs, confectionery moulds, dishes and various vases. Many of these objects had been taken to pieces and probably destined for restoration.

With the richer and more famous treasure of Boscoreale unfortunately emigrated and now in the Louvre Museum, this of the Menander is the best artistic silverware which the archaeological excavations of Pompeii and Herculaneaum have delivered to us, and in general also among the most beautiful examples known in ancient toreutics, the metal work which flourished between the end of the Republic and the beginning of the Roman Empire.

It is not always possible to establish with the data available whether material was imported from the Hellenistic centers of the East or copied from Hellenistic originals. Some have even put forward the theory that they are original pieces made in Roman workshops or perhaps in Southern Italy if not actually locally.

Silverware of the House of the Menander in Ancient Pompeii, goblet and chalice with olive branches

Aphrodite with Priapus

The taste of the ancients for painted marble, is represented by a statue of the first Imperial age found in Pompeii in January 1954 which portrays Venus completely naked, but "dressed" with a golden colour used for both the garment covering the intimate parts and the bracelet and necklace with which she is adorned.

The goddess has a slender body which acquires further agility from the helicoidal movement due to her bending forward to unlace a sandal. She has in fact raised her left leg, helped by a Cupid crouched at her feet holding the sandal and supporting himself in the instable movement against a Priapus who has lost his attribute. For analogy of movement it recalls a relief on the temple of Athena Nike built on the Acropolis of Athens in about 427 B.C. and which constitutes a lost echo of some Hellenistic and Neo-Attic realizations.

Aphrodite with Priapus, Greek marble. Prov. Pompeii, Villa of Julia Felix

Necklaces, bracelets, earrings and rings in gold. Prov. Pompeii

Goldsmith's Art

The Gold Collection in the Naples Museum, like the other material, includes objects from different places and ages.

It has been formed around two main groups: the first includes works in gold, only a few articles, which Charles III of Bourbon inherited from his mother Elisabeth Farnese in 1731; the second, the gold work from the archaeological excavations of Pompeii and Herculaneum, which the king himself started to collect in Capodimonte Museum. Thanks to the archaeological activity of the Vesuvian towns, this second group has continuously been increased until it has become the richer of the two. Consequently as far as it is possible to form a more or less precise idea of the epochs and the civilizations represented by the gold objects in the Museum, it is the passage from Greek to Roman goldsmithery which provides the greater amount of information. In considering the gold work found in Pompeii one should not forget the House of Menander where, in addition to the gold, an even richer collection of silver was found. Besides the two nuclei mentioned, and before the foundation in Southern Italy of other important museums, such as those of Reggio and Taranto, there were added all the sporadic discoveries in tombs in Italiot towns such as Armento, Canosa, Ruvo and Taranto itself. Anyway the best gold objects come from purchases of

Gold bulla from Pompeii

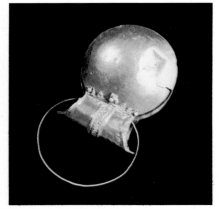

A necklace of ivy leaves and bracelets (the largest in the shape of an asp) all in gold. Prov. Pompeii

organic collections.

1) The Borgia Collection constituted in Velletri by Paolo Borgia during the XVIII Cent. and purchased in 1817. The material includes also objects from the Hellenistic East and so of a later period.

2) The Stevens Collection purchased in 1902. This includes objects coming, almost exclusively, from Cumae and found mainly as funerary furniture with other elements. This is a very important fact since these gold objects, easily datable, constitute a point of reference for gold work about which we are very short of data and information.

3) The Ricca purchase, including materials from the IV Cent. B.C. to the Hellenistic and Greco-Roman period, almost exclusively from Capua Vetere.

4) The Zona-Nobile purchase made in 1908 and including a very rich funerary furnishing from an Hellenistic tomb of Teano.

Its elements are very similar to those found in the Cumae tombs mentioned above.

5) The sporadic purchases and discoveries of Etruscan gold.

Less substantial than the others this group includes objects coming from discoveries near Cumae, Chiusi, Populonia, Vulci, Ruvo.

To this group belong the most ancient pieces among all the Museum's gold work, i.e. the funerary furniture of Cumaean tombs of Artiaco and Fondo Maiorana, respectively cremation and grave.

Oil lamp with horse-shoe shaped burners. Prov. Pompeii.

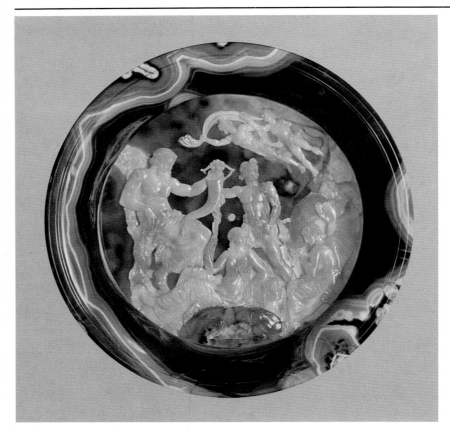

The Farnese Cup, cameo in sardonyx, diam. 0.234 m. Prov. Farnese Collection

Gorgon's head. External background

The Farnese Cup

Masterpiece of glyptic art of all times is a cameo among the biggest known, worked in the shape of a cup with a flat bottom and projecting edge, universally known as the "Farnese Cup". Probably executed in the Ptolemaic age in Alexandria of Egypt, this piece was a precious gift by Pope Paul II to Lorenzo dei Medici, from whom it definitely passed to the House of Farnese.

A gorgon's head with serpents round the neck and wings in the hair is engraved on the outside of the base, while engraved on the pale grey inner stratum which stands out on the richly veined, dark red background, is an allegorical scene which may represent the foundation of Alexandria, or - for most people - the personification of the Nile, the real benefactor of Egypt. The whole design of the scene follows the curved line of the bottom of the cup, but the attention is held by the river god seated on the left side with the cornucopia full of the fruits of the earth fertilized by him with the periodical inundations caused by the Etesian winds, personified by two male figures hovering above and blowing against the wind. Lower down in front of the god, half-naked and with agricultural tools in his hands, is Horus, he who taught men how to cultivate wheat, while at his feet, leaning against a Sphynx, is the maximum Egyptian divinity Isis. Forming a halo on the right are the nymphes Memphis and Anchirrhoe, i.e. the two Horae, daughters of Nile, with naked breasts, corresponding to the main seasons of Egypt, i.e. that of inundations and that of reaping, holding a cup and a horn. Behind them six ears of wheat.

This tendency to personify naturalistic elements, very common in Greco-Roman art, finds a famous reference in the reliefs of the Ara Pacis in Rome.

▶

Artemis, archaic imitation. I Cent. A.D. Prov. Pompeii

Terracottas

Most of the terracottas in the National Museum of Naples come from Southern Italian Regions (Campania, Lucania, Puglia and Abruzzi). Moreover their production was essentially of these regions and also when it developed farther North, as in Latium and Etruria, there is clear evidence of the importation from the South, if not of already made pieces, at least of the matrices for their production on a large scale. Consequently, one who attempts to follow a so humble, but very important type of art, and give it its proper place in the history of ancient art, must, obviously, turn to Magna Graecia and Sicily, particularly in view of its derivation from the relative Greek art. But of this latter, fortunately, ours retains only some of the influence because, once imported, it was clearly Italian taste which became imprinted upon it. And this is particularly important for the study of the art and customs of the regions mentioned, particularly considering the humbleness of the material used. In fact apart from the influence of the more "noble" art of sculpture which can be seen in it, it is the simpler aspects of every-day life which stand out, since most of the objects produced are tiny figurines connected in various ways with the archaic veneration of the dead and of the ancient divinities.

Fortune between the Lares. Bronze statuette, 0.22 x 0.36 m. Prov. Pompeii

Statuette of Venus. Bronze (gold for the jewels and silver inlays) 0.75 x 0.175 m. Prov. Herculaneum

Various Bronzes

Habituated as we are to knowing the past through the great traces of it which remain, and which are sufficiently strong to make an impression at first sight when encounted without being sought, we should force ourselves to take special notice when we come upon the more common objects of everyday life which belonged to our predecessors. This would appear to be the best way to get to know the progress and regression that Man has made in the various manifestations of life and through the centuries; the long journey and the evolution, sometimes slow and gradual, at other times rapid and apparently by sudden spurts, of our civilization. This is the only way to learn how to understand and therefore to love those who preceded us, so that once we have taken away the image of greatness and the air of mystery that veils the past, which is often known only through great catastrophic upheavals, we meet man with his everyday problems, surrounded by thousands of more or less useful objects with which his life identifies itself in one way or another. Thus the millennia of the past become real before our eyes, becoming shortened in a flash and the study of archaeology becomes really a study of us ourselves.

From this point of view the National Museum in Naples could really be considered as the only one in the world, at least for the Roman period, thanks, unfortunately, to the destruction-preservation of Pompeii, Her-

Fawn. Bronze 0,28 x 0.30 m. Prov. Herculaneum

culaneum, Stabiae and other ancient centres which Vesuvius caused with the famous eruption of 79 A.D. It is in fact the archaeological excavation of these towns which gave and still gives back to us an infinity and variety of objects preserved until now under masses of ashes and lapilli together with the human remains of the people who used them. Much of this material

Group of dogs biting a wild boar. Bronze . Prov. Pompeii: House of the Citharist. 1.22 x 0.50 m. I Cent. A. D.

would merit very different disquisitions if the task undertaken were not that of giving the hurried visitor a rapid outline; and within a limited space.

We find there a little of everything:

Mirrors with figured handles and with the disc decorated by graffiti of mythological subjects; statuettes of Italic Etruscan and Roman art representing various divinities (the most represented are the Lares, patrons of the house and of the quarter, and also Jupiter, Juno, Minerva, Mercury, Apollo, Diana, Hercules, etc.); (Hall XC showcases I-II and Hall XCI showcases I-II); ornaments for furniture such as small figured bronzes for bed- heads and feet (Hall XC show-case III); various objects including craters, jugs, amphorae and vases of different shapes and decorations (Halls XCII-XCIII); several and various oil-lamps, branched candlesticks, lamps and chandeliers, stoves, brazier holders and braziers. Among these latter the largest were certainly destined for public buildings, such as baths, before the more modern heating system with warm air circulating in the interstices of the walls was introduced; some smaller braziers, destined for private houses, had receptacles in which to heat water and cook or keep food warm (Hall XCIV). Also balances are numerous, with one or two plates of different shapes and sizes, and staters with figured weights, which gave the name to our "Roman", reproducing the features of the magistrate charged with controlling them.

Ithyfallic tripod. Bronze 0.47 x 0.57 m. Prov. Pompeii: House of Julia Felix. I Cent. A.D.

Ceramics: Fictile Vases

The art of manufacturing vases, before it became an artistic fact, was for all the ancient people a practical need of containers for thousands of uses, from which, with the improvement of techniques and refinement of taste they began to produce real artistic products, which often show the imprint, if not the signature, of great masters. Those who excelled in this art in the historical period, included all the peoples of the Mediterranean and particularly the coastal dwellers and the inhabitants of the Aegean Isles. These latter learned very early on, how to decorate vases with mineral colours and other vitrifying elements which gave brightness to the clay (the so-called shiny-paint) which started to be purified and worked using lathes, while they began to use special kilns for firing, abandoning the custom of baking the clay by covering it with fire.

In the archaic age (Mycenaean and Aegean period) the decoration used by Greeks consisted of very simple and stylized elements, often taken from flora and sea-fauna, used in panels or bands which gave it the name of "geometrical style".

Contemporaneously , i.e. around the VII Cent. B.C., also in Apulia a workshop for local ceramics was opened, the vases from which, not yet being turned on a lathe, were painted in red or black on the pale clay with bands of herbaceous designs, and schematic

Ceramics in geometrical design from Cumae (VII-VI Cent. B.C.)

73

designs of men and of animals, which suggest a derivation from Greek vases of the geometrical style mentioned previously. This supposition is supported by the migration of ancient races from the eastern basin towards Apulia.

And while this Apulian style of ceramics of VII and VI Cent. B.C. with its characteristic craters with handles, strips and roundels started to spread all over Southern Italy, the intensification of the traffic with the East brought into the centers of Magna Graecia vases produced in the North-East of the Peloponnese, usually very small ones, made with purified clay and with decorations of vine-tendrils, palmettes and spirals. The Naples Museum owns many of these vases known by the name of "Protocorinthian" from the necropolis of Cumae and collected in the Stevens Collection.

But starting from the middle of the VII Cent. B.C. there began to arrive, always from Greece, vases produced in Corinth, known as "Corinthian" and of which good pieces reached us through the old Collection of the Bourbon Museum. They spread not only in Southern Italy, but also in Etruria. The first "Corinthian" vases distinguished themselves from the "Protocorinthian" ones only by an accentuated taste for vegetable elements; but soon they differed from those in their storied decoration in zones or friezes with animals, monsters and finally human figures. And on these latter, while the empty spaces were abundantly filled with motives, inscriptions also began to appear. White and violet retouchings enlivened the whole. Contemporaneously in Etruria first (VII Cent. B.C.) and in Campania later (VI Cent. B.C.) a particular type of black ceramic (bucchero vases) appeared, often decorated with simple graffiti or in relief, while in Greece at the beginning of the VI Cent. B.C. the prevalence of Corinthian workshops was replaced by Athenian ones, the products of which became widely diffused owing to their perfection.

The Vase of the Persians

The most famous vase in the National Archaeological Museum in Naples comes from Canosa of Apulia where it was found with six others in 1851; this is a true Apulian masterpiece of the so-called Italiot pottery which flourished in South Italy. It was made around the middle of the IV Cent. B.C. and is known as the "Vase of the Persians" because of the figuration of the central body of the vase. It "narrates" with great richness of detail the preliminaries of the war conducted, and tragically ended, at Maradona (480 B.C.) against the Greeks.

In its complex the representation is no more than the exaltation and idealization of patriotic wars fought between unequal forces but won by the Greeks with divine help, sustained as they were by heroic national ideals against stronger and richer enemies.

The Crater of Ruvo with battle scenes between the Greeks and the Amazons

The Vase of the Persians, 0.59 x 1.15 m. Prov. Canosa di Puglia

Collection of Medals

The numismatic patrimony of the National Museum of Naples is really conspicuous (about one hundred thousand pieces). In this collection which was unclassified until 1864, when G. B. Fiorelli, director of the Museum at the time, after a previous but unsuccessful attempt, put it in order, publishing the relevant catalogue. It was added to by the Portici and the Capodimonte Collections, with the medals of the Farnese family and of Carafa (duke of Nola), the collection of medals from Monteoliveto, the gifts by Arditi and the purchases (among which the Stevens Collection) made by Fiorelli and de Petra. Thus almost all times and all countries are represented by pieces sometimes very common and of little value sometimes rare or quite unique and so of inestimable value. The pieces which may be seen by the visitor are of course very few examples chosen according to geographical and chronological criteria in order to give as rapid and faithful an impression as possible of all the material.

Storeroom in Cittanova
inv. n. 111315
End VI Cent. B.C. - Silver:
stater 7.84 gr; diam. 30 mm

D/AMI - Bull a.s. reflexed, on back:
grasshopper

R/ - same type in incuse

From Fiorelli catalogue n. 468
Rome 114-113 B.C. Silver: denarius;
3.73 gr; diam. 10.8 mm

D/ROMA - Female head
laureate a.d. with diadems and jewels
*behind ***

R/NM AEMILIO: Equestrian statue
a. d. on a three-arched bridge;
in which LEP

So-called Dancing Women, bronze with glass eyes, height 1.50 m. Prov. Herculaneum, Pisoni Villa

Young Satyr sleeping, bronze, height 1.15 m. Prov. Herculaneum, Pisoni Villa

Dancing Women

Known under the name of "Herculaneum Dancers", these five famous statues from the Pisoni Villa in Herculaneum, represent five women dressed in Doric peplums with stiff pleats hanging in folds; they are standing and are very similar one to another. They can just be distinguished in fact, by the slightly dissimilar movements of the arms, which confirms the hypothesis of a symmetrical arrangement, perhaps in special semi-circular niches, as might be deduced from the shape of the bases and from the similar destination of some marble replicas in the "Sallustian Horti". Not everyone agrees on the interpretation of these figures which, in spite of their stiffness, show a certain grace of movement. Perhaps it is this which has suggested dancers while some see them as hydrophores, that is to say, water carriers who have lost their attributes, the hydriae, or are waiting for them to be filled at the spring. Their similarity to other marble statues of women dressed in peplums, datable in the V Cent. B.C. suggests that these bronzes from Herculaneum may well be copies made in the I Cent. B.C. of Peloponnese originals.

Portrait said to be of Seneca, bronze, 0.335 m. Prov. Herculaneum

Portrait said to be of Seneca

There have been very many suppositions made on this portrait head from Herculaneum, in an effort to solve the riddle of the identification of the person represented.

From a casual comparison with a medallion of Maffei one thought immediately to Seneca, the philosopher-teacher of Nero; but the double herma of Berlin, having the names of Socrates and Seneca, cancels that hypothesis since it shows a completely different type. The crown of ivy which surrounds the head of the old man, even if present in only a few portraits among the approximately thirty known, has persuaded almost all the students to consider some Greek poet, and consequently there have been suggested the names of Philetas of Cos, Callimachus, Archilochus, Hipponax, Philemon. There seems to be no doubt nowadays that he was a Greek. He is in fact represented with a beard and might be associated with other portraits of Greek personages also found in Herculaneum. But it is the ivy crown which does not exclude the possibility that he could be an actor or an initiate to Dionysiac mysteries.

Apart from the importance, perhaps excessive, which has been given to this iconographic problem, which however is still unsolved, there remains the efficacy of this portrait, among the most noted of antiquity, also for the several copies in marble which are known. It is obviously a work of art of advanced realism, model of a style which developed in post-Alexandrine times and was continued throughout the whole Hellenistic period, when, in portraiture, either they tried to make up for the lack of resemblance to famous persons by creating them from pure and simple imagination, or, on the other hand, as in this case, resorted to a rough outline of the physical and psychological details, as was done in earlier years. The beard and the thick hair, in spite of the age, the dark but lively eyes, the deep furrows of the forehead and the thin cheeks giving even more emphasis to the cheekbones, and the lips slightly parted as if he were living an inner drama - these are the essential characteristics shown in the portrait of this famous but still unknown man who lived between the III and the II Cent. B.C.

Hermes resting, bronze, height 1.05 m. Prov. Herculaneum, Pisoni Villa

Statues of Fighters or Runners, bronzes, height 1.18 m. Prov. Herculaneum, Pisoni Villa

▼Statues of Deer, bronzes, height 0.96 m. Prov. Herculaneum, Pisoni Villa

© Publisher Carcavallo - Naples
Printing: Kina Italia Spa - Milan
Graphics Co-cordination: Studio Renzo Matino
Photographs: The Publisher's Archives - Klaus - Kina Italia Spa Milan